IN PROFILE

Great Press Barons

Graham Rickard

Wayland

In Profile

Women of the Air
Founders of Religions
Tyrants of the Twentieth Century
Leaders of the Russian Revolution
Pirates and Privateers
Great Press Barons
Explorers on the Nile
Women Prime Ministers
The Founders of America
The Cinema Greats
The War Poets
The First Men Round the World

First published in 1981 by
Wayland Publishers Ltd
49 Lansdowne Place, Hove
East Sussex BN3 1HF, England

ISBN 0 85340 881 5

Phototypeset by
Direct Image, Hove, Sussex
Printed in the U.K. by
The Cripplegate Printing Co. Ltd
Bound in the U.K. at
The Pitman Press

Contents

William Randolph Hearst

Hearst acquired many newspapers, and with them extraordinary power. For decades he wielded that power at the expense of those in American public life. When no sensational stories existed, he created them—he even manufactured a war. But the ultimate power he craved eluded him: not even the distorting mirrors of the Hearst press could suit his image to that of President of the United States.

'What is frequently forgotten in journalism is that if news is wanted, it has to be sent for . . . the public is even more fond of entertainment than it is of information.'

The pampered only son of a rich and powerful man, William Randolph Hearst remained a spoilt child for the whole of his life. When he wanted a newspaper to play with, his father gave him one, starting the largest chain of newspapers, magazines, press agencies, radio stations and film companies the world had ever seen. His newspapers and his money gave him immense power. At first he used this power for the good of the people, but he soon became addicted to power for its own sake, and was obsessed by the ambition of becoming President of the United States.

Ruthless and unscrupulous, Hearst used the sensational headlines of his newspapers entirely for his own ends. As *Time* magazine once said: 'No other Press lord ever wielded his power with less sense of responsibility; no other press ever matched the Hearst press for flamboyance, perversity and incitement to hysteria.'

Hearst was born in San Francisco, California, in 1863. His father, George Hearst, had made his fortune from prospecting and mining, and also owned

San Francisco before the 1906 earthquake. Hearst grew up in this rough and tough pioneering town.

several ranches. He was often away from home for long periods, and the young William Randolph was brought up by his mother Phoebe, who doted on him. She was a cultured ex-teacher and was determined that her 'darling boy' should have a good education.

Hearst grew up in San Francisco, which then was still part of the Wild West—a rough and tough pioneering town. There was no other large town for 1,000 miles; the citizens carried six-guns; and its vice, violence and corruption gave it a reputation as the most wicked city in the world, in which only the fittest survived.

Tours around Europe

Young 'Willy' was totally spoilt by his parents, who gave in to his every wish. When he was ten his mother took him on the first of many tours of Europe, which she, like most educated Americans of her time, saw as the cultural centre of the world. In Ireland he was appalled by the poverty he saw, and in England he formed his lifelong love of castles. His mother also gave him his taste for art, as they toured the museums and galleries of the continent. Mother and son returned to California loaded with paintings, sculptures and antiquities to decorate their home.

Six years later, after his second trip to Europe, Willie was sent to St. Paul's School in Concord, New Hampshire. It was the first time that he had been separated from his mother, and he hated the loneliness and strict discipline of a formal education. After two years, he could stand it no longer. At the age of eighteen, he returned home to continue his studies under private tutors.

By this time, George Hearst had opened even more gold and silver mines, and the family had become incredibly wealthy. Hearst senior became involved in politics, and accepted the failing local newspaper, the

This picture shows the Neptune Pool and Greek Temple at Hearst's castle at San Simeon, California.

Hearst's interest in newspapers soon became an obsession as he studied every aspect of newspaper production.

Examiner, as part of a debt, thinking it would help him in his election campaign for the Senate. The plan worked, and he later became Senator George Hearst. But the newspaper was of little interest to him.

In 1882 Willie entered Harvard University. By now he was a tall, slender figure, with large hands and feet and a girlish, high-pitched voice, which stayed with him all his life. Once again he disliked the routine and discipline of college life, and was a lazy student.

Expelled from Harvard

But he surprised everyone with his drive and determination when he was asked to take over the student magazine, the *Lampoon.* He sold advertising space to local traders and launched a circulation drive. The magazine, which previously had lost money, began to show a profit. Hearst began to take a new interest in his father's paper, the *Examiner,* which was sent to him every day from San Francisco. He studied the Boston and New York dailies and greatly admired the sensational style of Arthur Pulitzer's New York *World.* He frequently visited the office of the Boston *Globe* and studied every aspect of newspaper production. As his interest grew into an obsession, he wrote long letters to his father, criticizing the *Examiner*'s style and presentation.

At Harvard his pranks were getting him into trouble. Eventually, he was suspended from the university and went to Washington to study politics. When he returned, he continued his interest in newspapers—and his practical jokes. When he sent each of his tutors a specially-made chamber-pot, with their names inscribed on the inside, he was finally expelled.

At home again, he refused to be manager of any of his father's mines or ranches, saying: 'I want the San Francisco *Examiner*.' His father, who had already spent a small fortune to keep the paper alive, was very reluctant, but finally gave in.

Realizing that he lacked experience, Hearst went to New York, where he worked as reporter for the *World*. He fell in love with the paper and later copied its strange mixture of sensationalism and idealism. He could have had an easy life, doing whatever he wished, but his mind was made up. In 1887, at the age of twenty-three, he returned to San Francisco to take over the *Examiner*, which then had two telephones, one small old press, and a falling circulation.

The people's spokesman

The paper was losing vast amounts of money, but circulation and advertising both rose, as San Francisco began to sit up and take notice of his brash new style of reporting. Hearst had little time for ordinary news. He wanted the news which no one else had, even if he had to make it himself.

The paper praised itself each day as 'The largest, brightest and best newspaper on the Pacific Coast'. Hearst hired special trains to deliver the paper to outlying districts, gave away coupons for free trips in the bay and launched a dozen 'crusades' in the first year—for lower water-rates; against the power of the

Minneapolis Journal.]

The Spoiled Child.

WILLIE HEARST: "Guess this is my little boss. I bought him. Guess I can break him if I want to."

Many rival newspapers portrayed Hearst as a spoilt child who had the power to do as he pleased.

Southern Pacific Railroad; and fighting corrupt politicians. By the end of the year, he was recognized as the spokesman of 'the people', and had spent 300,000 dollars of the Senator's money.

When there were no sensations to report, Hearst created them. An *Examiner* reporter was assigned to have himself committed to an asylum for the insane, and write a heart-rending account of his experiences. As one editor said, 'What we're after is the "Gee-Whiz" emotion'. The recipe worked. By 1890 the paper was on its feet and showing a profit, but Hearst was not satisfied. He took a map of the United States, drew a ring around all the major cities and said: 'One day, a paper here, and here, and here.'

He had realized that he had the power to manipulate, as well as to protect the masses, and through them to dominate governments and influence their policies at home and abroad.

No shot is fired in Hearst's phony war

Father dies leaving fortune to wife . . . Hearst persuades her to sell shares . . . Buys New York Journal *. . . Obsessed with Cuban 'war' . . . National hysteria . . . Congress forced to declare war . . . Starts to build empire across America . . . Opens up radio stations and film studios . . . Ambition to become President . . . Hearst's newspapers attack public figures . . . Blamed for death of McKinley.*

Senator Hearst, disapproving of his son's extravagance and the *Examiner*'s reputation, refused to give William enough money to expand his empire. When he died, he left all his money to his wife, hoping that William would learn to mend his ways. But in 1895, he persuaded his ever-loving mother to sell the family shares in the Anaconda copper mine. She handed him the entire proceeds—seven and a half million dollars —and Hearst, 'the alcoholic of power', now had a licence to spend and do as he liked.

He immediately bought the first New York newspaper to come on the market, the *Journal*, and threw himself into the world of New York journalism 'with all the discreet secrecy of a wooden-legged burglar having a fit on a tin roof'. The *Journal* was losing money, but in a city with a population ten times larger than that of San Francisco, Hearst launched a circulation drive. 'Launching a newspaper without promotion,' he said, 'is like winking at a girl in the dark— well-intentioned but ineffective.'

Hearst's 'war'

The paper went to new lengths of sensationalism in its reports of scandals, murders and corruption. This style became known as 'yellow journalism' after the paper included a popular comic-strip, *The Yellow Kids.*

New York was forced to take notice of the new *Journal.* Although it lost money on every copy, the paper became more popular, and within a year was second only to the *World* in circulation.

In his battle with Pulitzer, owner of the *World,* Hearst decided that he needed something bigger than the usual stories of love, hate and power. What he needed was a real war, and if he could not find one, he would make one. He soon looked to Cuba, where a handful of rebels were opposing Spanish rule. The

Journal started printing stories of Spanish atrocities, of Cuban prisoners being beaten to death and fed to sharks.

Hearst became obsessed with the 'war', and made up stories, throwing away any respect for truth or principles. He sent the artist William Remington to Havana, paying him 3,000 dollars a month to illustrate stories of battles and atrocities. After seeing the situation for himself, Remington cabled: 'Everything is quiet. There is no trouble. There will be no war. I wish to return.' Hearst's famous reply was: 'Please remain. You furnish the pictures and I'll furnish the war.'

As national hysteria increased, Hearst tried to encourage American military involvement in an effort to step up the war. Thousands of people in America and England were persuaded to sign petitions in favour of the Cuban rebellion, but still Congress refused to be drawn into war with Spain. But then, in 1898, the American battleship *Maine* exploded in Havana harbour, with the loss of 260

Hearst used the explosion of the battleship Maine *to inflame public opinion against Spain.*

lives. The explosion was probably an accident, but Hearst immediately phoned the *Journal*'s editor, and told him: 'Please spread this story all over the front page. This means war.'

This incitement of public hatred led to two successes for Hearst: the *Journal* started selling one and a half million copies a day, and Congress was forced to declare war on Spain. The next morning's headline asked: 'HOW DO YOU LIKE THE JOURNAL'S WAR?' Hearst offered 1,000 dollars for the best idea to get the war off to a good start. As a gimmick to sell newspapers, Hearst had deceived, misled and tricked the American public into seething anger. No one listened when the Spanish Prime Minister commented: 'The newspapers of your country seem to be more powerful than the government.'

The Hearst empire

Hearst realized that more newspapers meant more power, and he started to build the vast Hearst chain, much of which still survives. He expanded first in the direction of Chicago, where the circulation battles grew into open gang warfare. Although Hearst did not directly control this activity, he turned a blind eye, and his silence condoned it. As long as he sold more newspapers, he did not care.

By 1927 Hearst dailies were also being published in Albany, Atlanta, Baltimore, Detroit, Milwaukee, Oakland, Omaha, Pittsburgh, Rochester, San Antonio, Seattle, Syracuse and Washington. The Hearst empire published twenty-five dailies in seventeen cities, with a combined circulation of over five million. His seventeen Sunday papers had an even larger circulation, and his magazines, including *Good Housekeeping, Cosmopolitan, Harper's Bazaar* and *Pictorial Review* were read by a third of America's population. Many millions more were reached by the Hearst telegraphic and syndicated news services,

A family photo of Hearst standing with his two sons aboard the liner Olympic *in 1922.*

FLASH GORDON by Alex Raymond

FLASH AND HIS FRIENDS DESPERATELY SEEK ESCAPE FROM THE CAVERN, AS THE GLACIER MONSTER SHUTS OFF THEIR AIR SUPPLY BY PLACING ITS GREAT TENTACLES OVER THE AIR-VENTS.

WITH A SMALL SOUNDING-DEVICE, FLASH AND ZARKOV MEASURE THE WALL THICKNESS BY ELECTRICAL IMPULSE.

AS TIME PASSES, BREATHING BECOMES MORE DIFFICULT AND THE COLD MORE UNBEARABLE. DALE, RONAL, KORRO, LUPI AND FRIA WATCH THE TWO MEN WITH HOPE FADING FROM THEIR EYES.

SUDDENLY ZARKOV SPEAKS-- "THE WALL IS THINNEST HERE. THERE'S A TUNNEL OR CAVE NEARBY!" "GOOD," BREATHES FLASH, "IF OUR POWER ONLY HOLDS OUT TILL WE BORE AN OPENING!"

BUT THE LAST RAY CHARGE FAILS BEFORE THEY ARE THROUGH-- "HATCHET," GASPS FLASH HOARSELY, "GET ME THE HATCHET!" "WE'RE LOST," GROANS ZARKOV, "THE OTHERS ARE UNCONSCIOUS ALREADY!"

FINALLY, ONLY FLASH REMAINS CONSCIOUS. SWEAT BATHES HIS BODY-- HIS BREATH COMES IN GREAT, LABORED GASPS--BUT HIS POWERFUL RIGHT ARM DRIVES THE HATCHET INTO THE ICE-- AGAIN--AND AGAIN--AND AGAIN.

THE WALL BREAKS THROUGH! AND FLASH PITCHES FORWARD ON HIS FACE, GULPING THE SWEET, PURE AIR INTO HIS TORTURED LUNGS.

~NEXT WEEK~ UNDERGROUND RIVER

Flash Gordon *was just one of the many cartoons syndicated by Hearst's telegraphic and news services.*

which sold news, features and cartoons (including *Flash Gordon*) all over the world. His other ventures included the motion-picture newsreel *Hearst Metrotone News,* a dozen radio stations, and *Cosmopolitan* motion pictures.

All the newspapers in the Hearst chain had the same look to them, as he stuck to the formula which he had discovered in San Francisco. The large headlines, sensational pictures, features and comic-strips were all ingredients in this formula, which usually neglected 'hard news' items in favour of lurid sensationalism.

After the Cuban War, Hearst was no longer satisfied with the power which his newspapers gave him. What he wanted now was real political power. So he started to promote himself in the same way as he had promoted his newspapers. He now had such a belief in his own abilities that he thought he could do anything, and from the start his eyes were fixed firmly on the White House. For the first time, the normally shy Hearst began to thrust his own name in front of the public, as he ruthlessly used his own newspapers to further his ambitions. Millions of readers were exposed to his name every day, and in one paper the name 'Hearst' appeared in three headlines on the same page.

Public figures attacked

As he made both friends and enemies in politics, he issued his papers with two long lists of public figures: those on one list were always to be attacked and criticized, and those on the other were always to be reported favourably.

At his command, the Hearst newspapers became more political in their outlook, running campaigns against the business monopolies who kept wages low and prices high, and pushing for badly-needed financial reforms. Public figures, including President McKinley, were ruthlessly attacked, and one editorial even claimed: 'If bad institutions and bad men can only be got rid of by killing, then that killing must be done.' Soon afterwards, on 6th September 1901, McKinley was assassinated, and Hearst was blamed by many for his death.

President McKinley signs the 1899 treaty with Spain. Hearst was blamed for his death.

Ultimate power eludes the 'King'

Elected to Congress . . . Fails in New York elections . . . Retires from public life . . . Supports Germany in 1914 . . . 'The Kaiser's spokesman' . . . Meets Adolf Hilter in 1934 . . . Witch-hunt against communists . . . Retires to San Simeon . . . Buys own film studio . . . 1930s Depression hits Hearst's newspapers . . . Maintains control of empire up to the end . . . Dies leaving a large fortune.

In 1902 Hearst stood for the first time as Manhattan Democratic candidate for Congress, and threw himself into the campaign with his usual energy and determination. He could have won with no campaign at all, but instead he brought in hundreds of helpers in a massive blaze of self-publicity, which included huge firework displays and packed meetings. He won by a huge majority, but was not a success in Congress. Although he professed to be a democrat, he found the process of democracy too slow, and did not understand the meaning of compromise or loyalty. He soon made enemies of all the leaders, and other politicians mistrusted his motives. This was the closest he ever came to achieving his Presidential ambitions, and his pride was sorely wounded when he lost the nomination for the 1904 election.

Not a man to give up easily, Hearst stood for Mayor of New York in 1905, but lost in a fraudulent ballot. In the following year he narrowly lost the election for the New York governorship, and again failed the mayoral elections in 1909. Many Democrats viewed him with real hatred, but he had great confidence in his personal popularity with 'the people', in his own political machine, and in the power of his newspapers. So great was this confidence, that he even toyed with the idea of forming his own independent party. His papers attacked his opponents with a new ferocity.

The Kaiser's supporter

By 1910, Hearst was politically dead. He retired officially from public life, but he could never give up his dream of the White House, and continued to dabble and interfere in politics for many decades. He also continued, through the columns of his newspapers, to influence public opinion and sway the course of events by his many campaigns. His longing

A scene from Citizen Kane, *a film based on the life of Hearst. Here Orson Welles, the star of the film, delivers an election speech.*

for the Presidency had caused him to lose both his principles and his self-control. He could not stand defeat. When he could not get his own way, he would sometimes fly into a rage, stamping around, screaming in his high-pitched voice, and breaking chairs and any other objects within reach.

At the beginning of the First World War, Hearst made himself the most hated man in America by defending Germany's position, attacking England, and insisting on American neutrality. The Hearst press was banned in England, France and Canada after printing such pro-German reports as 'The Allies Are Beaten'. The Germans, however, had his editorials translated into forty languages, and distributed them by the million as part of their propaganda campaign. Even after America declared war, he insisted that England was beyond saving, and that American troops should stay at home to defend American soil. He soon became known as 'the spokesman of the Kaiser', was regarded by many as a traitor, and was even put under surveillance by the Department of Justice.

Communist witch-hunts

In 1934, when war was brewing in Europe once again, Hearst went to Berlin and met Adolf Hitler. He tried to persuade him to stop persecuting the Jews, but his motives caused suspicion in America, where newspaper reports included photos of him with all the leading Nazis. He even started publishing a series of articles by Hermann Goering, but was forced to cancel them after nationwide protests. He publicly adored Mussolini, and once again opposed American involvement in a European war.

He also embarked on a vast anti-communist campaign, which turned into an obsessive witch-hunt, as his papers searched out and exposed supposed 'reds'.

Hearst shakes the hand of Adolf Hitler whom he met in Berlin in 1934.

Many of his victims were honest liberals, and this unscrupulous campaign was a negation of the democracy he claimed to defend. His great ally, 'the people', finally saw the millionaire for the dictator-like figure that he really was, and they turned against him. He was booed by 15,000 spectators at a mass meeting in New York and there were many demonstrations outside his newspaper offices.

His newspapers certainly did make him a lot of money. He was easily the nation's biggest spender. In 1922 his newspapers alone made a profit of twelve million dollars. He regarded these profits as his personal spending money.

The front of Hearst's guest house at San Simeon, California.

After 1926, he spent most of his time at his castle at San Simeon, California, where he lived more luxuriously than many monarchs. He also bought St. Donat's castle in Wales (although he had never seen it), a Bavarian-style village at Wyntoon, and homes in New York and elsewhere. He filled these, and several whole warehouses in New York with his fabulous collection of art treasures, mummies, dismantled Spanish castles, suits of armour and curiosities from all over the world.

San Simeon had started as his father's 40,000-acre cattle ranch. Hearst expanded it into his own private kingdom, protected by gates and sentries. He had a castle built there, with floodlit towers and accommodation for a hundred guests.

Movie mogul

His constant companion at San Simeon was the actress, Marion Davies. In 1903 Hearst had married another former actress, Millicent Wilson, and the couple had five sons. They had lived apart for many years, but his wife refused to divorce him so that he could marry Marion Davies. If he could not make

Hearst was determined to make Marion Davies the biggest star in the land.

Like the ordinary man in the street, the Depression years of the 1930's threatened to ruin Hearst financially.

Marion his wife, he was determined to make her a star. When his mother died, leaving him eleven million dollars, he plunged into the movie world, buying his own studio, and sparing no expense in his efforts to make Marion Davies the biggest star in the land, and himself the biggest of the movie moguls. Marion became his prize possession, and his newspaper reporters were forced to give her glowing reviews.

During the 1930s, the Depression threatened to ruin both Hearst and the Hearst empire. Many of his papers were closed, sold or merged, and finally Hearst gave up financial control of his empire. But eventually he recovered his finances, and his streamlined empire started to make vast profits again as the circulation of his newspapers increased as a result of the war which he had resisted so strongly.

The actor Orson Welles went to the top of his 'hate-list' when he starred in the famous film, *Citizen Kane*, which was based fairly closely on Hearst's life, showing a despotic newspaper tycoon as a lonely, frustrated and pathetic figure.

After Hearst reached the age of seventy, no one was allowed to mention death to him. He grew bent

Hearst's body lies in state in San Francisco.

and thin, and retired to San Simeon to act out his role as king-of-the-castle. Ill and weak, he refused to die, or to relinquish control of his empire, insisting that his papers still print the news that he wanted to read. When he finally died in Beverley Hills, in 1951 at the age of eighty-eight, his body was flown to San Francisco, and hundreds filed past to have a last look at the man who had shocked, manipulated and angered the nation for half a century. In his 125-page will, he left fifty-nine and a half million dollars, and the vast chain of newspapers which still survive and bear his name.

Dates and events

1863 William Randolph Hearst born in San Francisco, California (29th April).

1873 First trip to Europe, where he develops a taste for art.

1879 Starts at St. Paul's School in Concord, New Hampshire.

1881 Returns home to continue studies with private tutors because he disliked school life.

1882 Starts at Harvard University. He was expelled two years later.

1887 Takes over the *Examiner* in San Francisco, and within two years it had become profitable.

1895 Buys the New York *Journal* with money from his mother. Using numerous illustrations, glaring headlines, and sensational articles, the paper soon had an unprecedented circulation.

1898 Congress declares war on Spain after headlines on Cuba had appeared in the *Journal*.

1900 Following the success of the *Journal*, Hearst set up the Chicago *American*.

1901 Hearst is blamed for an editorial statement which led to the assassination of President McKinley.

1902 Becomes Democratic Congressman for Manhattan, and starts the Chicago *Examiner*.

1903 Marries Millicent Wilson, an actress.

1904 Loses nomination for Presidency; starts the Boston *American*.

1905 Stands for election as Mayor of New York, but is unsuccessful. Hearst buys *Cosmopolitan*, a monthly magazine.

1909 Fails in mayoral elections again and retires from public life.

1911 Hearst buys the *World Today*.

1934 Meets Adolf Hitler in Berlin.

1937 The Depression forces Hearst to assign control of his main holding company, American Newspapers Inc., to a banking-house trustee for ten years.

1941 Much of Hearst's vast collection of furniture and paintings is sold through department stores.

1951 Hearst dies in Beverley Hills, California (14th August).

Lord Beaverbrook

In each of his careers Beaverbrook achieved enormous success. A multi-millionaire by the age of thirty, he soon became the confidante of politicians and Prime Ministers. His newspapers became the mouthpiece for his isolationist policies. But when Britain refused to heed his propaganda and set itself against Nazi Germany, Beaverbrook, as a Government Minister, applied his energy to the new fight.

'I ran the paper purely for propaganda, and with no other purpose . . . In order to make propaganda effective the paper had to be successful. No paper is any good at all for propaganda unless it has a thoroughly good financial position.'

Lord Beaverbrook managed to compress three separate careers into one lifetime. As a young Canadian businessman, he brought off a series of spectacular deals which made him a multi-millionaire by the age of thirty. As an English politician, he became the friend of prime ministers and adviser of kings. His shadowy influence behind the scenes, intriguing and plotting, helped both to form and bring down governments. He and Winston Churchill were the only two men to sit in the British Cabinet during both World Wars, and it was Beaverbrook's energy and determination which provided the aeroplanes to win the Battle of Britain. But in his passport he described himself as a 'journalist', and it is as a newspaper proprietor that he is best remembered.

William Maxwell Aitken was born at Maple, Ontario, in 1879. His father was a Presbyterian minister who had emigrated from Scotland in 1864. The family was fairly well-off, and soon moved to

Beaverbrook standing outside the house in Maple, Ontario where he was born.

Newcastle, New Brunswick—a small town set among hills, forests and salmon rivers, far from any large city. Max had ten brothers and sisters, but he was always a loner, 'the cat that walks by itself', as he later said. He was a clever boy, but restless and impatient, with a mischievous grin that stayed with him for the whole of his life. His large mouth gave him the nickname of 'moccasin mouth', and one of his friends told him: 'God couldn't make your mouth any bigger without removing your ears.'

He was extremely lazy at school. Instead of concentrating on his books ('too many words', he complained), his mind was often far away, thinking up pranks or new schemes for making money. He had a very large paper-round which he 'farmed-out' to other boys, who worked for him on commission. At the age of thirteen he launched his own newspaper, the *Leader,* and he became a local reporter for other papers, collecting commission by selling subscriptions. His sister said: 'Max did not make money because we were poor. He made money because he liked making money.'

Ambition to be rich

When he left school, Max failed to get into university, and worked in a Newcastle drugstore for one dollar a week. Throughout his life, he needed an older or stronger man to spur his ambitions, and he now met the first in a long series of heroes. R. B. Bennett, a local lawyer, impressed Max so much that he decided to make law his career, and he entered Bennett's firm as a clerk. He soon had his first taste of politics when he ran Bennett's successful campaign to become an alderman. He was also selling life-insurance policies at the time, and Bennett's partner soon complained: 'After he had been in my office for about a month, I was not sure whether he was working for me, or I for him.'

After a brief and unhappy spell in law school, Max drifted aimlessly for two years, making money from bowling alleys, cargoes of frozen meat, and insurance policies, and losing it at poker and dice. In 1900, after running into debt, Max made the decision that was to change his life: at the age of twenty-one, he decided he wanted to be rich, very rich. As he changed from selling insurance to selling company-bonds, he could not have chosen a better moment. These were the years of the great financial boom in Canada.

In Halifax, Max set up the Royal Securities Corporation, the first big bond-selling company in eastern Canada. The company was very much a one-man band, with Max doing all the work. Buying and selling companies soon brought out another of his talents—his flair for publicity. Needing something

In 1900 Beaverbrook (second right) decided that he was going to be very rich. By 1907 he was a dollar millionaire.

Bonar Law, with Beaverbrook's help, became leader of the Unionist Party in 1911.

more than his own persuasive tongue, he started supplying the local press with stories which pushed his companies into the news, and often increased their value. He also started ventures in the West Indies, and by 1907 he had achieved his first ambition —he was a dollar millionaire. But he was still restless, and after providing for the welfare of his parents and family, he decided that Halifax was too small for him.

In 1906 he had married Gladys Drury, whose father was a distinguished and influential figure in Canada. Max admitted that he was a difficult man to live with. He tended to turn his friendships on and off as he needed them, and marriage did not change his nature. The Aitkens' honeymoon showed him at both extremes. After showering his new wife with gifts, he gave her a brief taste of New York's dizzy social life. Then he took her to the West Indies, where he largely ignored her, spending his time looking into various business ventures.

Conservative M.P.

When they moved to Montreal, Max spent his time travelling all over Canada, spending as little as one night at home in two months. For a time he became an investment banker, but soon returned to selling bonds, and in 1908 went to London for the first time. One of his customers in London was Bonar Law, who was later to have a powerful influence on his life.

Back in Canada, Max saw the country as one nation rather than a collection of provinces. In a series of vast merger operations, he began to bring small companies together to form large national corporations.

Bored with high finance, he and Gladys left for England in 1910, little realizing that they were never to live in Canada again. When he arrived in London, he was unknown, and his political ambitions were scorned by those who saw him as 'the little Canadian adventurer'. Needing a new hero, he remade the acquaintance of Bonar Law, a prominent figure in the Unionist Party, and declared: 'I am going to pick out a good, sound Liberal seat and turn it over to the Conservative Party.' Law helped him to find a suitable constituency—Ashton-under-Lyne, near Manchester—and Max threw himself into the fray. He had already mastered the techniques of propaganda, and he was soon selling himself to the voters as he had once sold bonds and companies. In the 1910 election campaign, he hired brass bands, and he and Gladys gave an 'at home' for 3,000 local women.

Political mediator

After winning by a small majority, he took his seat in the House of Commons, but found the processes of democracy too slow and quiet for his impatient nature. He did, however, make a point of getting to know all the public figures of the day—Stanley Baldwin, Sir Samuel Hoare, David Lloyd George and Winston Churchill. As a reward for his services to the party, and to persuade him to stay in British politics, he was offered a knighthood. Within a year of his arrival in the country, the unknown Canadian was Sir Maxwell Aitken, M.P.

He bought a house in Cherkley, Surrey, which he fitted out with a tennis court, swimming pool and private cinema. Frustrated by parliamentary debates and endless committees, he soon found himself a new central role in politics, as mediator and go-between for opposing groups. His back-stage direction was largely responsible for Bonar Law becoming leader of the Unionist Party.

Winston Churchill (left) and Stanley Baldwin were two public figures that Beaverbrook made a point of getting to know when he entered British politics.

Max gains a title, starts a Crusade

Unofficial Canadian diplomat in England . . . Starts his own newspaper for Canadian forces . . . Brings down Asquith government . . . Given a peerage . . . Buys Daily Express . . . *Made Minister of Information in 1918 . . .* Express *prospers . . . Starts* Sunday Express *in 1919 . . . Helps make Bonar Law Prime Minister . . . Buys* Evening Standard . . . *Empire Crusader . . . King's adviser.*

In 1914, at the outbreak of the First World War, Parliament was adjourned, and Max felt that he could play no useful role in England. He went to Canada on a recruiting drive, where he made the acquaintance of Prime Minister Borden, who asked him to return to England as unofficial Canadian ambassador and observer. As 'Canadian eye-witness', he assembled vivid war-stories and distributed them to news correspondents. He went to France to see the war for himself and started a newspaper, *The Canadian Daily Record,* for the forces serving in England and France. He was the first to bring in official photographers and film crews. When the British Press wanted a picture of a tank (then a new weapon), they had to borrow one from his office. He also started the Canadian War Records Office, in which he hoarded every tiny scrap of military information. All this activity sprang from Max's own enterprise and initiative, and displayed his well-developed talents for publicity.

Beaverbrook's coat of arms. Rudyard Kipling helped Beaverbrook in its design after Lloyd George had offered him a peerage.

During the First World War, Beaverbrook (left) became unofficial Canadian ambassador and observer.

In England, Asquith's position as head of a half-hearted government seemed secure, but he was criticized by Lord Northcliffe's press for the fruitless slaughter of a badly-organized war. In 1916, Max sensed the situation, and made full use of it. Intriguing and plotting behind the scenes, he pushed events and personalities in the direction he wanted. Within days, Asquith resigned, never to hold office again, and the Liberal Party was broken for ever. A coalition government took over, with Lloyd George as Prime Minister. Max was later to say that the biggest thing he had ever achieved was 'the destruction of the Asquith government, which was brought about by an honest intrigue'. Beaverbrook's friend and biographer, the historian A. J. P. Tylor, called this episode 'the biggest merger operation of his life'.

The grateful Lloyd George, against the wishes of King George V, offered Max a peerage. After feigning reluctance, he accepted, and Sir William Maxwell Aitken became Lord Beaverbrook. In fact, he was delighted. He had recently bought the *Daily Express,* and his new title put him on a par with the two great Press Barons of the day, Northcliffe and Rothermere. He took his title from a stream near Newcastle where he used to fish as a boy, and his friend, the author Rudyard Kipling, helped to design his coat of arms.

Beaverbrook's flair for publicity and propaganda made him the ideal choice for the post of Minister of Information.

The *Daily Express,* under the editorship of Blumenfeld, had been the official newspaper of the Unionist Party, and Beaverbrook had been subsidizing it, and using it, for several years. When it was threatened with closure because of its huge debts, Max bought the paper for £17,500. His original intention was to use it purely for propaganda, to back up his own ambitions and intrigues. He soon began to interfere, directing the paper's editorial policies.

When he bought the *Express,* Northcliffe asked him: 'How much are you worth?' When Beaverbrook replied 'Over five million dollars', Northcliffe commented: 'You will lose it all in Fleet Street.' In fact he had to spend two million pounds of his Canadian resources before the paper started showing a profit.

In 1918, with the war still not over, Lloyd George made Beaverbrook Minister of Information. He saw propaganda as 'the popular arm of democracy', but not all politicians agreed with him. When the Foreign Office, guarding secrecy, denied him access to information, he flew into a rage and threatened to resign. His temperament was never suited to public office, and he was glad, at the end of the war, to give up his post and regain his independence.

A comic-strip

Paying the highest wages in Fleet Street, Beaverbrook attracted a talented team of journalists to put forward his favourite policies, and to boost the *Express*'s circulation. He was a great believer in prosperity, and in 1922 declared that the *Express* stood for 'More life, more hope . . . more money . . . more work . . . more happiness.' He saw peace as essential for national prosperity, and pushed for a policy of non-interference abroad. He believed that England should remain in 'splendid isolation' relying on the colonies of her Empire for trade and industry.

A scene from 'Rupert Bear', *the first comic-strip to be introduced into an adult newspaper.*

Beaverbrook relaxes in the sun on the French Riviera after playing tennis with two of his Society friends.

His strongly independent line often angered the Unionists.

As he poured money into the *Express,* it became a bright and lively paper, attracting readers from every social class. He tried to ensure that it was enjoyable to read. In 1920 he introduced the first children's comic-strip in an adult newspaper—'*Rupert, the Adventures of a Lost Little Teddy Bear*', which was the invention of the wife of one of his staff. In the Second World War, when the shortage of newsprint caused most comic-strips to be dropped, Beaverbrook insisted that '*Rupert Bear*' should continue, and he still appears every day in the *Daily Express.*

A London paper for free

In 1919 he started the *Sunday Express.* The paper cost him half a million pounds in the first year. It was a near disaster; he tried one editor after another before the paper got off the ground. He later wrote: 'The corpses of *Sunday Express* editors were spread up and down Fleet Street in every direction.' He even tried editing the paper himself, until he found the right man, John Gordon. The *Sunday Express* became a unique family newspaper with a very large, and profitable, circulation.

Beaverbrook was soon at the centre of a new political intrigue. This time, after Lloyd George's resignation in 1922, he managed to manoeuvre his hero, Bonar Law, into No. 10 Downing Street as Prime Minister. But his triumph was short-lived; Law resigned due to ill-health within a year, and soon died. His dying words to Beaverbrook were: 'You are a curious fellow.' Beaverbrook's political influence died with Law, and he soon made an enemy of Stanley Baldwin, the new Prime Minister.

From now on, Max's only power lay in his newspapers. In 1923 he decided that he needed a London

Beaverbrook addressing a Conservative Party meeting. He campaigned vigorously for the ideal of Empire Free Trade.

paper as an extra voice. To achieve this, he bought the entire Hulton Press for £4,500,000, detached the *Evening Standard* from the group and sold the other papers to Rothermere for the total original price. He had gained his new paper for nothing. During the next decades, his newspapers ran colourful campaigns for his own radical, and eccentric, policies. Their columns attacked the new Co-operative societies, and supported such issues as higher wages and Scottish Home Rule. Although he did not agree with Sir Oswald Mosley's fascist ideals, he remained friendly towards him. His vendetta against Baldwin, though, was a terrible example of the way in which he used his newspapers to harass and seek to destroy a public figure who would not bend to his will.

The Empire Crusader

His greatest campaign was for the romantic and unrealistic ideal of Empire Free Trade, which he championed with an almost religious enthusiasm. He donated £25,000 to start a campaign fund, and advertized the Empire Crusade Register in 1929. His newspapers were pressed into the service of the Crusade. (To this day the Empire Crusader appears on the front page of the *Daily Express*.) He campaigned up and down the country, enlisting supporters and fighting by-elections. He even threatened: 'It is my purpose to break up the Conservative Party if it does not adopt the Empire Free Trade policy.' The Crusade finally ran out of steam and was forgotten, as more important issues dominated the political stage. But at one point many people saw Beaverbrook—head of the United Empire Party—as the next Prime Minister.

The depression of the 1930s saw an incredible circulation battle, as all the major newspapers fought for increased sales. The *Herald, News Chronicle,*

The Empire Crusader *(top right corner) has appeared on the* Daily Express *front page for over fifty years.*

Daily Mail and the *Express* all tried to outdo each other in offering free gifts to subscribers. Books, clothing, insurance and sets of cutlery were all given away as the four papers spent £60,000 a week to attract new readers. The *Herald* just beat the *Express* to become, for a few days, the first newspaper to sell two million copies a day. Beaverbrook was amused by the battle, but kept a careful eye on the quality, as well as the quantity, of his papers' output. He read every edition of his three papers every day, comparing them with his rivals' papers, counting advertisements and exclusive 'scoops', and pestering his editors on the telephone with a constant barrage of criticism.

His prestige and influence were shown in 1936, when King Edward VIII recalled him from a trip to America. The King wished to marry Mrs Simpson, an American divorcee, and he wanted Beaverbrook's advice and help. Beaverbrook did his best to delay matters, and to mediate with Parliament on the King's behalf, but without success. The King was forced to abdicate in December 1936, and left for France to marry Mrs Simpson.

Beaverbrook opposed British involvement in a European war. Here he is stating his views on B.B.C. radio.

Max joins Churchill against the Nazis

Most people were more worried by events in Germany, where Adolf Hitler was in power. Not wanting another war, Beaverbrook wrote in the *Express*: 'The British Empire minding its own business is safe. The British Empire meddling in the concerns of the Balkans and Central Europe is sure to be embroiled in war, pestilence and famine.' He made a broadcast on B.B.C. radio in favour of the policy of isolation. He was invited to Berlin to meet Hitler, who convinced him that he wanted friendly relations with England. But he allowed his desire for peace to cloud his judgement, and in 1938 the *Express* declared: 'Britain will not be involved in a European war this year, or next year either.' He kept hoping until the last moment; even when Hitler invaded Poland, he suggested: 'Poland is no friend of ours.'

When war was declared, however, Max threw all his energies into winning it. He was sent to America to sound out President Roosevelt's feelings about the war, and the two men immediately became good friends. Back in England, he sensed dissatisfaction with Chamberlain's leadership and once again assumed his role as back-stage manipulator. Within days Chamberlain had resigned, to be replaced by Winston Churchill, Beaverbrook's last great hero. The two men became constant companions.

Spitfire fund-raiser

After talks with Stalin in Moscow, Beaverbrook accepted the post of Minister for Aircraft Production, responsible for providing the poorly-prepared R.A.F. with enough aircraft to defend Britain. His ministry disregarded all the usual Civil Service rules and protocol, and was run in the same way as his newspapers. His impatience to produce more aircraft *at once* made him unpopular at times, but he swept aside all resistance.

Working seven days a week, he launched the Spitfire Fund, which raised thirteen million pounds. Air Chief Marshall Sir Hugh Dowding commented: 'The effect of Lord Beaverbrook's appointment can only be described as magical . . . The country owes as much to Beaverbrook for the Battle of Britain as it does to me. Without his drive behind me, I could not have carried on throughout the battle.'

Churchill's adviser

Beaverbrook was now recognized as the second most powerful figure in the country, and took on even more responsibilities. He became a member of the war cabinet and of the defence committee, and was made Minister of Supply. He was always the centre of a whirlwind of activity. After a bad air-raid, he would appear on the scene, urging the workers to rebuild, and restore production. After resigning from the Ministry of Aircraft Production, he was made the first-ever Minister of State, and moved to No. 12 Downing Street. When Hitler's deputy, Rudolf Hess, arrived in Scotland to promote peace, Beaverbrook interviewed him.

Towards the end of the war, he became Churchill's personal envoy to Russia and America, but lost much of his real power in England. When he was made Lord Privy Seal, he became a member of the real cabinet of 'the men who saw Churchill after midnight'. He was involved in every aspect of national life. But, at the end of the war, Churchill's Conservative Party lost the election and Beaverbrook's active political career was finished forever. The working classes were suspicious of the millionaire newspaper owner, and he was forced to retire from public life.

The strain of the war-years showed itself as the bouts of asthma he had suffered from childhood grew worse. For the sake of his health he bought a house at

Lord Beaverbrook in his office when he was Minister for Aircraft Production.

The Ministry of Aircraft Production under Beaverbrook's direction had the task of providing the R.A.F. with enough aircraft to defend Britain.

La Capponcina in the south of France, and others in Jamaica and the Bahamas, where he spent most of the winter months. In Canada, he became Chancellor of the University of New Brunswick, where he spent two months every autumn, involving himself in the running of the university.

As the circulation of the *Express* rose to four million, he was content to keep firm control of his papers. He also busied himself with writing modern history books, including *Men & Power: 1917-18*, *Friends* and *The Divine Propagandist*.

WORK LIKE A BEAVER. AND DAM THE NAZI HORDES.

Beaverbrook's drive and energy was used as an example for others to follow during the war.

Wartime photograph of the Daily Express *building.*

Beaverbrook showed himself at his worst in his personal vendetta against Lord Mountbatten, which lasted from 1942 until 1962. After an initial friendship with Mountbatten, he turned against him when the Chief of Staff insisted on dealing with Churchill direct, rather than through Beaverbrook. At a dinner party, he accused Mountbatten of murdering thousands of Canadians at Dieppe, and said: 'I'm going to destroy you.' Over the next two decades his newspapers systematically attacked Mountbatten at every opportunity, even calling him a traitor. In 1953, a *Sunday Express* editorial said: 'Lord Mountbatten, the last and worst of all the pro-consuls we ever sent to India, his misjudgements destroyed us ... In all the world we have fewer worse enemies.' When the Press Lord died, the *Daily Express* asked Mountbatten for his comments: 'Well, the kindest thing I can do for Lord Beaverbrook is to make no comment whatever.'

The final years

For most of his life, Beaverbrook was very rich, and he enjoyed his wealth. He spent freely on his many houses and was fond of cigars and champagne. Once, before he grew bored with racing, he spent £300,000 on racehorses. Then he turned his attention to yachts and private aircraft instead. He gave away most of his money to various charities, and was always generous to his family and friends. He hated paying taxes, and made sure that his money went to charity rather than to the taxman after his death. As he grew older, he 'retired' many times, but in fact refused for an instant to give up control of his papers.

His first wife, Gladys, had died in 1927, and in 1963, crippled with gout, he secretly married Lady Christopher Dunn. The next year, Lord Thompson gave him an eighty-fifth birthday dinner with 600

Despite 'retiring' many times, Beaverbrook refused to give up control of his newspapers.

guests. He died two weeks later, and his ashes were taken to New Brunswick after a memorial service in St. Paul's Cathedral. His great rival, the *Daily Mail* paid tribute to him: 'Hated, feared, admired, adored, Beaverbrook was a great chuckling twentieth-century personality, a political mischief-maker, brilliant propagandist, newsmaker as well as getter.'

His son, Sir Max Aitken, inherited control of the Beaverbrook newspapers, but in 1977 they were taken over by an international shipping and construction company, Trafalgar House, who removed the name Beaverbrook from the papers. Today only the impish face of 'the Beaver', sculpted by Epstein, gazes down on the hall of his Fleet Street building to remind journalists of the control which he once held over his kingdom.

Dates and events

1879 William Maxwell Aitken born in Maple, Ontario (25th May).

1892 Launches his own newspaper, the *Leader*, and becomes a local reporter for several others.

1900 Sets up the Royal Securities Corporation in Halifax to sell company bonds.

1906 Max marries Gladys Drury.

1907 Achieves his first ambition by becoming a dollar millionaire.

1910 Leaves Canada for England and is elected Conservative M.P. for Ashton-under-Lyne.

1911 Knighted as a reward for his services to the Conservative Party.

1914 Prime Minister Borden of Canada appoints Max unofficial Canadian ambassador and observer in England.

1916 Max helps bring about the resignation of Asquith's government and is rewarded with a peerage from George V.

1918 Lloyd George appoints him Minister of Information.

1919 Max starts the *Sunday Express*.

1920 Introduces the first children's comic-strip in an adult newspaper — *Rupert Bear*.

1923 Takes over the *Evening Standard*.

1927 Gladys Drury dies.

1929 Max sets up the Empire Crusade Register to promote Empire Free Trade.

1936 King Edward VIII seeks Max's advice over his marriage to Mrs Simpson.

1942 Max starts his vendetta against Lord Mountbatten.

1945 Sent to America to discuss the war with President Roosevelt.

1963 Secretly marries Lady Christopher Dunn.

1964 Dies shortly after his eighty-fifth birthday (9th June).

Axel Springer

'The papers of the Springer house are not loyal to the Government—they are loyal to the Republic': in a sentence Axel Springer reveals the purpose of the press he controls. His mission is to see the two halves of Berlin re-united; his method is to use the unprecedented influence of his newspapers on people and politicians alike. Many see the danger of that influence, but few have dared to condemn it.

'I devote myself to you,
With heart and hand,
Land full of love and life,
My German fatherland.'
(Traditional German song, quoted by Herr Springer at the opening ceremony of the Axel Springer Publishing House in 1966.)

The skyline of Berlin is dominated by Axel Springer's massive publishing house, in the same way as he himself dominates the modern German Press. The steel, glass and concrete skyscraper looms defiantly over the Berlin Wall, just 180 metres (200 yards) from Checkpoint Charlie, and Herr Springer's office overlooks both East and West Berlin. Axel Springer's declared mission in life is to see the two halves of the city re-united, and he has built up the greatest concentration of press power in the world to promote his personal ideals. In the true tradition of Hearst and Beaverbrook, he realized that a high readership was the key to newspaper power, and he was the first German publisher to seek a mass circulation amongst his fellow countrymen. He now commands over seventy per cent of West Berlin's daily newspaper readership, and over forty per cent

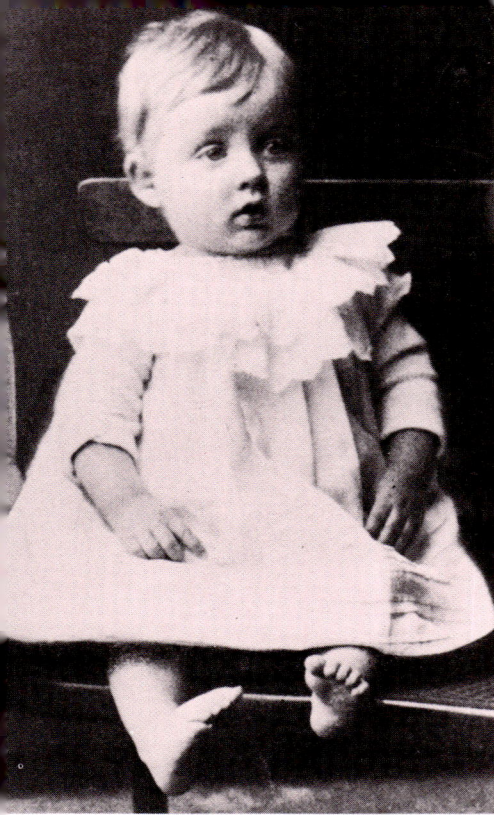

This portrait of Axel Springer was taken when he was about eleven months old.

of all dailies sold in West Germany. His monopoly is often criticized as a 'huge and worrying influence', and there have been protests against the power which he wields over German politics, but few public figures would openly dare to condemn him.

Axel Caesar Springer was born in a suburb of Hamburg in 1912. His father, Heinrich, owned a small weekly newspaper, the *Altonaer Nachrichten,* and Axel grew up in a world of newsprint and printing presses. After studying at the local school, the *Realgymnasium* in Hamburg-Altona, he took up apprenticeships with various provincial papers to learn the trades of printing and publishing. He also trained as a journalist with the W.T.B. news agency before returning to work on his father's paper. This thorough training in all aspects of newspaper production was later to stand him in good stead.

Licensed to publish

During the Second World War, Springer managed to keep out of the Nazi Party, without openly opposing it. He was also lucky enough to escape being called up for service in the German armed forces. This was partly because of ill-health, but also because his father's printing-shop was playing an important part in the war-effort—it had an army contract to print light literature and romantic novels to cheer up the soldiers at the front.

At the end of the war, the Allies' occupying forces banned all publications in the German language, including newspapers and magazines. Radio programmes, films, and even concerts and cabaret shows in German were also banned. The Nazi propaganda machine had taken over almost all the media, and it was felt that Germany needed to start afresh with a 'clean slate' if it was ever to have a well-balanced and responsible Free Press. Licences were then issued to those publishers who could prove that

A Nazi propaganda picture from the Second World War.

Springer bought control of Die Welt *in 1953.*

they had a record of independence—a difficult task, as most of them had been forced to promote official Nazi propaganda during the war.

Lord Barnetson (until his recent death a Press Baron himself, as chairman of United Newspapers) was then a member of the British Control Commission responsible for issuing licences. Queues and delays for licences seemed endless, and the Commission members grew impatient as they interviewed hundreds of applicants, each with the same story of Nazi oppression and political innocence. Lord Barnetson remembered his first meeting with Axel Springer, in his Hamburg office in 1945: 'He had come to see me with a view to restarting his old family firm of Hammerich & Lesser. I had been interviewing other aspiring publishers all day, and had become rather weary of circumstantial rigmaroles about persecution by the Nazis, for some of them seemed to have suffered little, if at all. At any rate, Axel Springer was ushered in, and I asked him: 'Well, who's been persecuting you?', to which he offered the unexpected but credible response: ''Women!'' '

A national publisher

Springer's direct approach paid off, and he soon had his licence. Within a few months, he launched *Hor Zu* (*Listen*), a magazine giving details of all the radio programmes. From this small beginning, *Hor Zu* became the biggest-selling magazine in Germany (it still is) and the money which it made provided the foundation for his future empire. Lord Barnetson later commented: 'It is true that Axel Springer was lucky with his licences . . . But licences or not, he would have come to the top in any case.'

Springer started publishing a local afternoon paper in Hamburg, *Abendblatt.* He got on very well with the British, because, he says, they shared a love of

43

horses. The British had established *Die Welt,* a quality national daily paper, on English lines, as an example to the German Press of how a newspaper should be run. *Die Welt* was a great success, and in 1953 the British decided that the time had come to hand over the paper to a German publisher. Axel Springer bought control, and immediately became a national, rather than a local publisher. This decision has been criticized, but Lord Barnetson claims that 'in the early fifties, Axel Springer was clearly one of the most imaginative and most courageous publishers of his generation, and many of us would have been very sad to see our brainchild passed on either to professional mediocracies or to people without the resources to keep the thing alive.'

Springer working on his paper, the Abendblatt, *in Hamburg in 1948. Today it is the largest-selling afternoon paper in West Germany.*

An empire rises from the ashes

Buys Die Welt *for one million pounds . . . Germany's biggest publisher . . . Doubles sales . . . Powerful influence of* Bild Zeitung *. . . Feared by most politicians . . . Press monopoly . . . Forced to sell magazines . . . Demonstrations by students . . . Business genius . . . Uses new technology . . . Wants to re-unite his country . . . Meets Khruschev in Russia . . . Immense wealth . . . Admires Britain.*

At the age of forty-one, Springer became Germany's biggest publisher when he paid about a million pounds for *Die Welt*. Although serious in tone and content, the paper has a lively feel to its layout and presentation of the news. It was already highly regarded, and widely read by the professional and intellectual classes when Springer took it over, but he has more than doubled its circulation without reducing the quality of the paper. Today it is published in Hamburg, Essen and Berlin, and has only one competitor as a quality national daily. *Die Welt* has the widest news coverage in Germany, with foreign correspondents in sixteen countries. Conservative in its outlook, it has kept its reputation for honest and responsible journalism. In 1967 the University of Missouri's School of Journalism paid tribute to the paper's coverage of world affairs, when they awarded Springer an Honor Medal for 'distinguished service in journalism'.

Feared by politicians

As his empire grew, however, not all his papers showed the same high standards of fair and unbiased reporting. *Bild Zeitung* is West Germany's only mass circulation daily tabloid. It is similar in style to the *Daily Mirror* but completely outdoes the *Mirror* in sensationalism. When you buy it, the news-vendors warn: 'Mind you shake the blood out!' Its popularity is based on its basic recipe of violence and sex. The paper's policies are far more right-wing than those of *Die Welt,* and the paper is designed to appeal to the eye rather than the intellect. *Bild Zeitung* identifies itself with readers' prejudices, exploiting and encouraging them. With a circulation of almost five million, it is the only paper that many Germans read, and its glaring headlines and emotional articles have a tremendous influence.

This newspaper stand in West Germany probably sells many of Springer's newspapers.

Axel Springer uses this influence to the full. The paper has consistently attacked those government ministers who do not conform to Springer's ideals and many have since found themselves out of office. He himself refers to the paper as his *Kettenhund*—his dog on a chain—and few politicians wish to see the chain removed for the hound to leap at their throats.

Press monopoly

With *Bild Zeitung* for the masses and *Die Welt* for the serious-minded, Springer owns two of the only three national dailies in the Federal German Republic. He also owns the only two national Sunday papers, *Welt am Sonntag* and *Bild am Sonntag*. The *Hamburger Abendblatt* is now the largest-selling afternoon paper in the country, and the *Berliner Morgenpost* has the highest circulation of any paper. *Hor Zu* is still by far the most popular magazine in Germany, and Springer also owns two evening papers—the *Mittag* in Dusseldorf and the *Berliner Zeitung.* At one time his empire used to include a rich collection of glossy weeklies, aimed at every section

In 1967 Springer met Golda Meir and Moshe Dayan, two important politicians, while in Israel.

Springer's massive publishing house dominates Berlin's skyline.

The city of Berlin is split between East and West Germany by the Berlin Wall.

of German society—*Bravo* for teenagers, *Twen* for those in their twenties, *Jasmin* for newly-weds, and *Eltern* for parents. But in 1968, after a government-appointed commission warned of the dangers of a press monopoly in Germany, which stifled diversity of opinion, Springer was forced to sell these magazines.

In the previous year, there had been another sign of the growing discontent with Axel Springer's stranglehold on the German Press. Springer's papers had offered little sympathy when a student was shot during a protest demonstration against the Shah of Iran's visit to Berlin. Outraged, the students retaliated with mass demonstrations outside his newspaper offices, and tried to prevent the distribution of his papers. Their concern was justified—even *Der Spiegel,* Springer's main competitor, is printed on his presses.

New media technology

No other publisher in post-war Germany has showed Springer's business genius, or his ability to appeal to a mass audience. His annual turnover from his newspapers and audio-visual companies is £120,000,000 and his success is largely due to his willingness to use new media technology. Since 1955, his publishing centres have been linked by teletypesetter devices, and in 1952 he was the first to use Telephoto to receive pictures direct from the Helsinki Olympic Games. His publishing empire now has its heart in Berlin, in the enormous Axel Springer Publishing House, which cost £25,000,000 to build, and contains all the latest print technology. When it was opened in 1966, Springer gave an emotional speech at a ceremony attended by the Federal President Heinrich Lubke and Mayor Willy Brandt. He declared: 'The papers of the Springer House are not loyal to the Government—they are loyal to the Republic', and he re-affirmed his mission to re-unite his divided fatherland.

To further his aims, he even went to Russia to discuss Germany's future with Khruschev. But his cold reception produced bitter anti-Russian feelings in him. He frequently makes violent anti-communist outbursts. It is because of his strong political beliefs that the concentration of press power in his hands is considered by many to be so dangerous. He claims not to directly interfere with the editorial policies of his papers, but editors know that they are expected to follow his line of thought on any issues which they report.

In appearance, Axel Springer is an elegant, handsome man. He has a reputation of being irresistible to women and has been married four times. Immensely wealthy, his collection of fine houses includes one in Berlin, two in Hamburg, a London base in Mayfair, two villas on the North Sea island of Sylt, and a chalet

Axel Springer relaxes at home with his son, Raimund.

Springer is often seen with some of the world's most influential people. Here he is with Henry Kissinger.

in the fashionable Swiss resort of Klosters—Prince Charles' favourite skiing location. All these are filled with art treasures and antique furniture from many countries.

Springer has retained an admiration for Britain, and all things English. Following the style of the English upper classes, he has his clothes made in Savile Row, and owns a large racing stable. In 1978, when *The Times* was about to cease publication because of an industrial dispute, he wrote a letter to the paper, calling it 'the queen of Fleet Street', and wished it a speedy return to normal publication.

More interested, perhaps, in publishing an opinion than in the objective reporting of events, Axel Springer is a true Press Baron—the first in Germany's history. Unlike Hearst and Beaverbrook, his strong political views have not so far tempted him to enter into politics directly. But his monopoly of public opinion is far mightier than theirs ever was, and his influence in Germany is easily as great as that of any democratically-elected leader. The extent of his influence is unrivalled by any proprietor in world newspaper history.

Dates and events

1912 Axel Caesar Springer born in Hamburg, West Germany.

1945 Successful interview with Lord Barnetson to obtain a publishing licence: *Hor Zu (Listen)* launched.

1952 Axel's papers pioneer the use of Telephoto by receiving pictures direct from the Helsinki Olympic Games.

1953 Buys control of *Die Welt,* the national newspaper set up by the British after the war.

1955 The Springer publishing empire is linked by teletypesetting machines.

1966 Axel Springer Publishing House opened in Berlin.

1967 Mass demonstrations outside his headquarters following the death of a student during the Shah of Iran's visit; awarded Honor Medal.

1968 A government commission warns of a press monopoly in Germany, and Axel is forced to sell four of his magazines.

49

Rupert Murdoch

From Australia to Britain to America, Murdoch has swept aside all obstacles in his bid to establish his newspaper empire. Scarcely a year passes without an addition to his list of publications; and tradition is never allowed to threaten the profitability of his new acquisitions. Despite criticisms of his journalistic methods, Murdoch, Prince of Fleet Street, has now set in his crown the brightest of jewels, *The Times*.

'The muck-raking tradition in popular journalism is an honourable one.'
'I don't like a fight for a fight's sake, but if you get into one, it's good to win it.'

Clutching a newspaper in one hand, and a balance-sheet in the other, Rupert Murdoch is the perfect example of the modern newspaper tycoon. Bristling with energy and enthusiasm, his whirlwind career has covered three decades and three continents, and his tough, ruthless tactics have often made him the centre of controversy. Starting with a dying little newspaper in the outback of Australia, with his aggressive methods he has built up a business organization which includes not only newspapers, but television and radio stations, book publishing, films, airlines, transport, paper-making, mining, gambling and land development. This soft-spoken Australian has made himself the master of the take-over bid, and in the last thirty years, there has not been one year in which he has not bought something, started something, or fought someone. As the new prince of Fleet Street, he has introduced a keen edge to newspaper competition, in his relentless drive for circulation and profits.

A young Rupert Murdoch leans out of a train window with his father Sir Keith Murdoch.

Born in Sydney in 1931, Keith Rupert Murdoch was named after his father, Sir Keith Murdoch, who was one of the founders of the modern Australian Press. Starting with the *Melbourne Herald,* Sir Keith built up a successful newspaper empire, created the Australian Associated Press, and founded the national newsprint industry.

'Red Rupert'

The young Murdoch was educated at Geelong Grammar School, Victoria, but did not like the school, and kept to himself. He was always in the bottom half of the class, and was not good at sports—he was too lazy to take an interest. But he had already gained the nickname of 'Red Rupert' for his rebellious socialist ideals and the headmaster later remembered him as 'Oh, that little nuisance.'

His left-wing views later developed at Worcester College, Oxford. He did, in fact, sit on the committee of the Oxford University Labour Club. He still found it difficult to concentrate on his studies, but here he formed real friendships for the first time, and mixed with a smart set of intellectuals which included Shirley Summerskill and Gerald Kaufman.

His freedom gave him a new self-confidence, but

Sir Keith Murdoch (left) was one of the founders of the modern Australian Press.

Murdoch used the Adelaide News *to expose corruption and injustice. Here he is on a fact-finding mission to the outback.*

his father was outraged by his left-wing tendencies, and threatened to take him away from the university. As his final exams approached, he had little chance of graduating; but his tutor and friend, Asa Briggs, took him on a six-week holiday and crammed enough information into him to enable him to get a second-class degree in economics.

His father had died in 1952 before Rupert left Oxford. The young graduate decided to gain some practical newspaper experience before returning home, and went to London to ask Lord Beaverbrook for a job. For two months he worked as a sub-editor on the *Daily Express* for £10 a week, learning all there was to know about page-presentation and layout. One of the staff later described him as 'the cheekiest and busiest little whipper-snapper ever to sit at the end of the table.'

Boardroom fighter

When he returned to Australia, he was immediately caught up in a financial battle to keep his father's publishing empire intact. But most of the papers had to be sold to pay for death duties, and the young Murdoch was left with only a fifty-seven-per-cent share of one paper, *The News,* in Adelaide. The paper was losing money and was faced with a take-over bid by the *Advertiser.* Murdoch successfully fought off the bid, and proved himself to be a tough boardroom fighter as he built the paper into a profitable concern.

The *Adelaide News* became a radical, campaigning paper, using the power of the press for the public good, by exposing corruption and injustice.

Murdoch soon started to find new outlets for his ambition and energy. His first real coup was his sudden purchase of Channel 9 T.V. in Adelaide. Single-handed, he started the S.T.V. Corporation

Sir Frank Packer at the time of selling his papers to Rupert Murdoch in 1972.

with a tiny borrowed capital of a quarter of a million pounds which he soon paid back from the companies' profits.

In 1958 he had the idea of starting a new national paper which would give details of the television and radio programmes in every state of Australia. He flew to America to study how the idea worked there, and insisted on visiting Las Vagas, the world's greatest gambling centre. Gambling is part of the Australian way of life, and Rupert Murdoch is one of its biggest addicts. He won and lost a small fortune in a few days.

His first marriage began to break up under the strain of his high-pressure career, but he pushed ahead with his plans for expansion, buying the Perth *Sunday Times.*

A national newspaper

He now felt ready to take on the tougher newspaper world of Sydney, which was dominated by three aggressive characters—Frank Packer, John Fairfax and Ezra Norton. After Murdoch bought a television station south of Sydney, Packer sold him a string of failing papers, including the Sydney *Daily Mirror,* in the belief that they would be a millstone around his neck, and would eventually bankrupt him. But the *Daily Mirror* gave Murdoch the 'foot in the door' which he so badly needed. The *Mirror*'s circulation began to rise, and after the first two difficult years, Murdoch became unstoppable. In 1972 Packer finally admitted defeat and sold his papers to Murdoch. The *Mirror* soon became the mainstay of his organization, and his years in Sydney taught him how to survive the toughest newspaper competition in the world.

In 1962 he realized a long-standing dream of the Murdoch family by starting to plan the country's first

The Daily Mirror *was the first Sydney newspaper bought by Murdoch.*

national newspaper, the *Australian*. It was a very courageous decision, in the face of every possible difficulty. The average Australian is not over-interested in news of the other states in the country, and the distribution problems were enormous in a country whose major cities are separated by thousands of miles. The paper went into production in 1965. Typeset by computer in Canberra, the plates were then flown to printing centres in Melbourne, Brisbane, Adelaide and Perth. In bad weather, Murdoch could be seen on the runway at Canberra, urging the planes to take off, as he fought to keep the paper alive. The *Australian* has had a troubled history, with sixteen editors in fifteen years, but it is now firmly established as a profitable concern, with a wide readership and a reputation for quality reporting.

Murdoch hopes that the *Australian* will help to give his country some kind of national identity, which he thinks is lacking at the moment.

Murdoch's presses roll around the world

With his Australian empire firmly established in the hands of a dynamic young management team, Murdoch turned his ambitious eyes towards London's Fleet Street. Ever since his Oxford days, he had quietly dreamed of owning the *Daily Mirror,* and he started to invest his profits in I.P.C., its parent company. Then, in 1968, the *News of the World,* the world's biggest-selling newspaper, gave him the opportunity he needed. Robert Maxwell, a millionaire socialist M.P. who owned the profitable Pergamon Press, made a take-over bid for the paper. Its proprietor, Sir William Carr, whose family had been associated with the paper since 1890, phoned Murdoch's Sydney office to ask for help. Murdoch flew in from Australia and the directors of the News of the World Organization agreed to form a consortium with Murdoch as chief executive. They thought they were adding his company, News Ltd., to the News of the World Organization, but in fact he was doing the opposite. Rupert Murdoch had gained a foothold in Fleet Street.

The battle had lasted for months, and almost every

Larry Lamb speaking at a press conference soon after he had been appointed the new editor of the Sun.

Sir William Carr (left) congratulates Murdoch on becoming chief executive to the News of the World *. Robert Maxwell looks on.*

day the clash of personalities between Maxwell and Murdoch made front-page news. It was one of the toughest take-over battles in history. At the age of thirty-seven, Murdoch had made the biggest catch of his career, and from the start he made it clear that his aim was to expand the paper.

He took an active part in running the paper, and with new editors and managers from his organization, the paper soon became more profitable. The paper still relied on its old recipe of sensational reports of sex, scandal and violence, wide sports coverage and simple political comment. Murdoch, now known as 'Rupert the Bear', had grown much less radical in his political ideals which made it easier for him to accept the political tone of the *News of the World*.

Maxwell defeated again

In the following year he defeated Robert Maxwell for the second time in an even more remarkable coup. The *Sun* (originally the *Daily Herald*) had lost twelve million pounds in six years, and its owners, I.P.C., decided to close it down as a hopeless proposition. Robert Maxwell put in a bid for the paper, but a few days later Murdoch emerged as the new owner.

I.P.C. might well have imagined that the *Sun* would prove a millstone around Murdoch's neck, which would drain away both his energy and resources. Instead the paper rapidly became a major rival to their own best-seller, the *Daily Mirror*.

He found a brilliant editor for the bright young paper, Larry Lamb, under whose direction the paper has gone from strength to strength. Recently the *Sun* overtook the *Daily Mirror* in daily sales, and Murdoch now owns the two biggest-selling newspapers in Britain. But he has made many enemies in Fleet Street, and attracts a good deal of criticism from those who claim that he debases journalism for profit, and that he interferes with the editorial policies of his papers.

The attacks continue, and Murdoch is not untouched by the criticisms. He told an interviewer: 'I am just as thin-skinned as anyone else. I don't welcome dislike, but if you're doing properly the role of publisher you don't get all the respect you and your wife would like.'

American chain of papers

Not content with his success, he started to expand his English operations, buying a large block of shares in London Weekend Television (L.W.T.) and soon gaining control of the company. But the Independent Broadcasting Authority, the controlling body of independent television, objected to this. They said that it was against the rules to buy himself in through the back door without a licence, and demanded that he give up his position. As well as L.W.T., he has interests in Independent Television News, a transport company and paper-making concerns. After buying shares, he made an unsuccessful bid for Beaverbrook Newspapers, and later considered buying the *Observer*.

Rupert Murdoch relaxing at home with his wife and child.

Murdoch being greeted by Jimmy Carter (then President of the United States of America) at the White House in 1980.

In the 1970s, after long fights with the print unions, and continued attacks on his business and journalistic methods, he became disenchanted with Britain, and looked across the Atlantic towards an untried market. In 1973 he bought the morning and evening papers in San Antonio, Texas. Few people could understand this move, but it was another example of his foot-in-the-door technique. Within two years he made himself a force to be reckoned with in American journalism.

When he started the *National Star,* a tough weekly tabloid, it was his biggest gamble yet. The project had cost a fortune, and it was a difficult market to break into. Murdoch poured his energy into the paper, and within a few months its circulation had soared past anyone's expectations. He later paid thirty million dollars for the *New York Post,* a staid and fading paper, and made it pay its way by changing it into a more sensational and eye-catching product. He increased his hold on the city by acquiring *New York Magazine, New West Magazine, Cue,* and *The Village Voice.* His sensationalism has alienated many former readers of the *New York Post.* This used to be a liberal paper, but in the 1980 election campaign it solidly supported Ronald Reagan, and criticized Carter's administration at every opportunity.

Political influence

The multimillionaire international newspaper magnate seems to have forgotten the socialist idealism of his student days and, although generally conservative in his outlook, he seems to have no real political allegiances. No politician would be wise to rely on his support, which can easily change to opposition. Most leading politicians have been invited to his farm at Cavan, near Canberra, where he quite

Rupert holds a copy of the The Times *at a press conference announcing that he had just become the new owner of the Times Group of newspapers.*

openly demands policy changes in return for his support.

In 1972 he went on a boatride around Sydney harbour with Gough Whitlam. Murdoch backed Whitlam, who won a landslide victory in the election.

Parliamentary protests

In 1981, Murdoch was once again in the headlines when he was offered *The Times,* the *Sunday Times* and the *Times* supplements. Ownership of these would give him control of both ends of the British newspaper market, controlling thirty per cent of daily sales and thirty-five per cent of the Sunday readership. His bid was greeted with howls of protest and a three-hour emergency debate in the House of Commons. M.P.s shook their heads and proclaimed that it would be 'a bad day for British journalism if it [*The Times*] fell into the hands of this tycoon who has in the past used his papers to put forward his own political views.'

Murdoch gave many guarantees of editorial independence as a condition of his bid. He feels sure that he can make the papers pay without lowering their standards of journalism, and says: 'Nothing is more unhealthy than an unviable newspaper which lives off rich families.' When asked how he would make *The Times* profitable, he replied: 'By putting a lot of hard work into it as well as getting more advertising, selling more copies, and doing all we can to get it right.' He is the world's most successful newspaper publisher, and if anyone can make *The Times* pay, he can. But it remains to be seen whether he will keep his promise and retain the paper's long tradition of independence and impartiality.

Away from the boardroom, Rupert Murdoch is a quiet, very ordinary man. Apart from work and gambling, he does everything in moderation. He only really relaxes when with his second wife Anna and

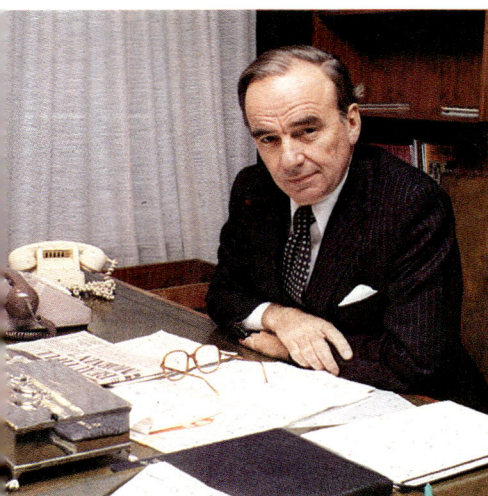

Rupert Murdoch at work in his London office.

their three children. As well as his Australian home at Cavan, he has a suite in London's Bouverie Street, and a house in Epping. He has a chauffeur-driven Mercedes, but usually goes to work on the tube; he once tried a helicopter, but found that it took longer. He is a tough man to work for, and one managing director once said: 'I like Murdoch to be at the end of a telephone . . . I like him to be nice and far away.' In his office, he sits behind a huge antique desk, handing out decisions at an incredible rate, and somehow manages to keep in touch with every part of his vast organization.

Still only fifty years old, Murdoch, with his abundant energy, manages to double his company's profits every seven or eight years on a spiral of expansion. Some say that his papers have lost some of their original fire and adventurous spirit, and that Murdoch relies too heavily on his well-worn formula for success. It certainly seems as if his press empire has reached saturation point, and it is difficult to see where he can turn next to find an outlet for his ambition. However, it is doubtful if Rupert Murdoch would share that opinion.

Dates and events

1931 Keith Rupert Murdoch born in Sydney, Australia.

1952 Father dies while Rupert is still at Oxford University.

1958 Goes to America to develop his ideas for a new national newspaper in Australia.

1965 Launches the *Australian*, which is distributed around the country by air.

1968 Becomes chief executive of the *News of the World* in London after a battle with Robert Maxwell.

1969 Rupert defeats Maxwell again to take over the *Sun*.

1972 Frank Packer sells his papers in Sydney to Rupert.

1973 Buys newspapers in San Antonio, Texas, starting his American chain of papers.

1980 His *New York Post* supports Ronald Reagan in the Presidential elections.

1981 Rupert buys *The Times* and *Sunday Times* despite the protests of British M.P.s.

61

Glossary

Abdicate   To renounce the throne.
Alderman   A senior town councillor.
Atrocity   An act of extreme cruelty.
Coalition   An alliance, for example between political parties.
Coup   A sudden, successful act.
Despot   A ruler with unrivalled power.
Eccentric   Odd behaviour.
Envoy   A diplomat.
Fascist   A person with extreme right-wing views.
Flamboyance   Behaviour intended to attract notice.
Hysteria   Wild excitement, usually of a large number of people.
Incitement   Deliberately provoking an act.
Intrigue   An act done in secret.
Magnate   A person with much wealth or power.
Mogul   An important or powerful person.

Monopoly   A situation where a single person or firm has a dominant position in a particular industry.
Pestilence   A deadly, infectious disease.
Propaganda   The organized spreading of particular ideas or opinions.
Protocol   A set of rules for formal occasions.
Radical   A person who seeks far-reaching changes, especially in politics.
Syndicate   A news agency that sells articles to several newspapers for simultaneous publication.
Socialist   A person who believes that property should not be privately owned, but in the hands of the State.
Tabloid   A newspaper with pages about 30 cm (12 in) by 40 cm (16 in), with an emphasis on photographs and a sensational style.
Tycoon   A businessman of great wealth.
Vendetta   A prolonged quarrel.

Further Reading

On journalism:

Newspapers: The Power and the Money by Simon Jenkins (Faber, 1979)
Dangerous Estate: The Anatomy of Newspapers by Francis Williams (Longmans, 1957)
Pressures on the Press: An Editor looks at Fleet Street by Charles Wintour (Deutsch, 1972)
Journalism Made Simple by David Wainwright (W.H. Allen, 1972)

On Hearst:

Citizen Hearst: A Biography of W.R. Hearst by William A. Swanberg (Longmans, 1962)

On Beaverbrook:

Beaverbrook: A Study in Power and Frustration by Tom Driberg (Weidenfeld & Nicolson, 1956)
Beaverbrook by A.J.P. Taylor (Hamish Hamilton, 1972)

On Murdoch:

Rupert Murdoch: A Business Biography by Simon Regan (Angus & Robertson, 1976)

Index

Picture acknowledgements

The publisher would like to thank all those who provided illustrations on the following pages: Beaverbrook Papers, House of Lords Records Office 24, 25, 38 (both); Daily Express Syndication Department 32 (above); Internationales Bildarchiv 47 (above); John Topham Picture Library *front cover* (above right), 26; Keystone Press Agency *front cover* (below left), 52 (below), 55, 57, 58, 59, 60, 61; © King Features Syndicate Inc. 13; London Express News and Features Services 34 (above), 39; Malcolm S. Walker 4, 17, 18, 19, 22, 29, 33, 34 (below), 37, 40, 44, 46 (below), 48, 50, 53, 56; National Film Archive 16; News Limited of Australia 52 (above), 54; Photri 6, 7 (above), 11, 14, 18 (above); Press Association *front cover* (below right); Private source 42, 49; Radio Times Hulton Picture Library *front cover* (above left), 9, 27, 28, 30-31, 32, 36; United Press International Photo 7 (left), 12, 20; Zefa 46 (above), 47 (below).